The Spirit of Family

David Graham

2

Alice Attie

Laura Wilson

Call it a clan, call it a network, call it a tribe, call it a family.
Whatever you call it, whoever you are, you need one.

—JANE HOWARD

James Newberry

Mary Ellen Mark

Toba Pato Tucker

Duane Michals

9

Leonard Freed

11

Jodi Cobb

Milton Rogovin

Hank Thomas and Bayeté Ross-Smith

Al and Tipper Gore

The Spirit of Family

WITH GAIL BUCKLAND AND KATY HOMANS

Henry Holt and Company   New York

Tipper Gore

The Spirit of Family

We live our lives in the emotional universe of our families. Love, like gravity, is always there, holding us securely in place—even as we fall free.

In the beginning, when first there is light, we are entirely dependent on the warmth and nurturing energy of a bright star at the center of the circle that marks our days. The more we grow, the wider our gyre. But the pull of our origins is always, always a powerful if invisible force. At every stage of life, those who are closest to us—parents, brothers, and sisters; then husbands, wives, and partners; then daughters and sons—all tug at our orbit and bend our direction, some insistently, others more faintly.

Families are reality, not invention. They are always present, always remembered, and always hoped for. They are much more than mere associations of individuals. They have a transcendent integrity of their own. We shape and nurture our families and they shape and nurture us. And wherever we go in life, our families live in our hearts.

The two of us have long been interested in every aspect of family life, and in early 2001, we began researching a book about the dramatic changes occurring in American families. We soon realized that words alone would be insufficient to our task, so we decided to explore this endlessly fascinating topic using images as well. Two books ultimately emerged from our efforts: this collection of photographs and a book called *Joined at the Heart: The Transformation of the American Family*. In both, we have attempted to capture the essence of what family is and how families are changing.

With these remarkable photographs, we try to show that the spirit of family is neither abstract nor invisible. It can be felt in the indentation of a child's fingers in his foster mother's cheek; seen in the radiant smiles of aging sisters whose bonds with each other are always vital; and heard in the clamor and laughter of three generations crowded around a picnic table.

Each of the images in this book tells a story about family. And each of the families, whether happy or unhappy, is unique. But the spirit of family is in many ways the same for all of them—and for all of us. It is a spirit that can seem fleeting and elusive amid the bustle and noise of our daily lives. But it can be framed clearly in a frozen moment of time captured by a photographer who blends skill with patience and good fortune.

Seeing clearly is the job of photographers, and many of those whose work is included in *The Spirit of Family* have used the camera as a tool to help them understand the dynamics of family life and to explore the impact society has on these essential relationships. Indeed, many of America's finest photographers have long believed that the greatest subject for their craft is not wars or the dramatic events of history, but the way people interact with one another—how they touch; how they hold their children in their arms; how they get through their day with all the stress, strains, and joys that life hands them; how they deal with personal pain, illness, loss, and death; and how one generation relates to the next.

In the course of preparing this book, we reached out across the United States and approached the widest possible range of American photographers, from established masters to graduate students in photography. We specifically asked every photographer we contacted to review the images they've recorded that address the subject of family. The response was overwhelming, and we were pleased to discover that some of the most passionate and important—and, in many cases, unpublished—American photography dealt with just this topic.

In all, we looked at more than 15,000 photographs to find the 256 images that we believe best convey the truth we are trying to show. Every style of photography is included, from the snapshot aesthetic of Gerald Cyrus, Edward Keating, and Sylvia Plachy, to the socially committed photojournalism of Jane Evelyn Atwood, Donna Ferrato, Eugene Richards and Joseph Rodriguez, to the highly personal compositions by Tina Barney, Lee Friedlander, Sally Mann, and Nicholas Nixon. Even photographers who are known for their stylized portraits, such as Annie Leibovitz, also sometimes take wonderful, candid photographs of their parents and friends.

Included here are works by major art photographers, *National Geographic* photographers, and a group of women photographers who have raised the notion of "photographing their families" to an unprecedented level of lyricism, poetry, and perception, such as Maude Schulyer Clay, Lauren Ronick, and Jennette Williams. We found that although most photographers take photographs of their own families, they often do not exhibit or publish these pictures. And one of the many joys of selecting and organizing these images has been the discovery of powerful photographs by relatively unknown artists.

These pictures show contemporary American families of all shapes and sizes. They demonstrate that the spirit of family encompasses traditional forms as well as dynamic new relationships that also provide love and security. As these photographs suggest, we are all defined partly by our relationship to our family of origin and partly by our experience of the inevitable passages of loving, working, playing, and aging. The portraits in this book depict all stages of life—from birth to young adulthood, from marriage to old age. And while some of the families pictured in these pages present themselves to the camera as a strong coherent whole, others are clearly in crisis.

Our simplest goal in preparing this book is to share the experience of other people's lives. But we also believe that these images reveal the ability of photography to connect people visually to the vast range of human emotion and the rich variety of relationships that bind us together in families. Photographs often have a visceral and instantaneous impact, one that's more potent than words. To our eyes, the images here have an almost magical ability to capture the powerful forces that draw people together and sustain them.

The theme of this book is the personal connections and common passages that almost all families experience. We hope these photographs convey the resilience of people facing the challenges of family life in contemporary culture, the ways that family is being redefined by a rapidly changing society, and the enduring qualities shared by most families. Nothing is more essential than the relationships we have with our loved ones, and in these pages we draw upon photography in an effort to bring the spirit of family to life.

Al and Tipper Gore

June 2002

Birney Imes

Mitch Epstein

Malerie Marder

That Love is all there is,
Is all we know of Love.

—EMILY DICKINSON

Gregory Bojorquez

Ruth Kendrick

25

Lauren Greenfield

Kenneth Jarecke

Eli Reed

Doug DuBois

Catherine Opie

Susan Meiselas

Justin Kimball

Joel Sternfeld

Constantine Manos

Arlene Gottfried

Nan Goldin

Jim Goldberg

Bruce Davidson

Debbie Fleming Caffery

Childlike, I danced in
    a dream;
Blessings emblazoned
    that day;
Everything glowed
    with a gleam;
Yet we were looking
    away!

—THOMAS HARDY

William Albert Allard

There is a sacred, secret line
  in loving
which attraction and even
  passion cannot cross,—
even if lips draw near in
  awful silence
and love tears at the heart.

—ANNA AKHMATOVA

Laura Letinsky

Anthony Barboza

Let flesh be knit, and
each step hence go
famous.

—SYLVIA PLATH

Bruce Davidson

Paul D'Amato

Edward Keating

William Albert Allard

Laura Straus

Sally Mann

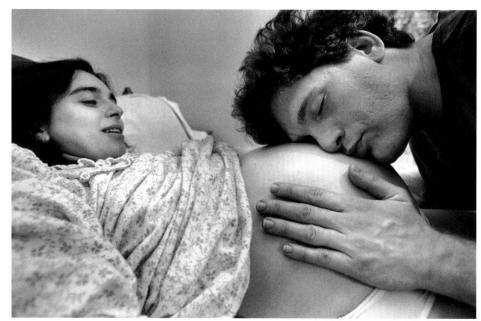

Eugene Richards

Arlene Gottfried

Making the decision to have a child is momentous.
It is to decide forever to have your heart go walking
around outside your body.

—ELIZABETH STONE

And when our baby stirs and struggles to be born
It compels humility: what we began
Is now its own.

—ANNE RIDLER

Jim Goldberg

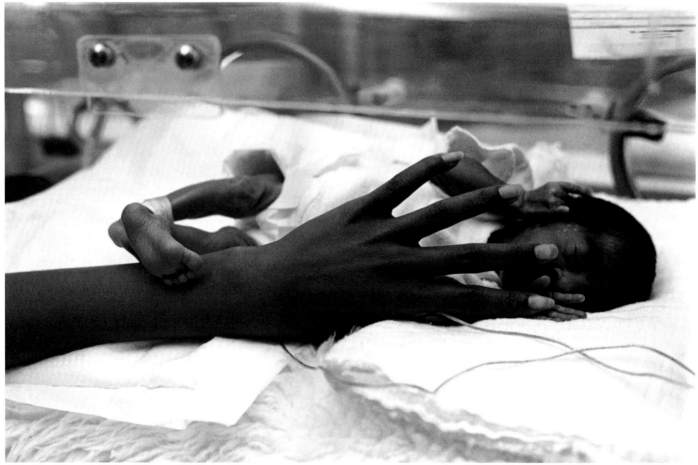

David Hurn

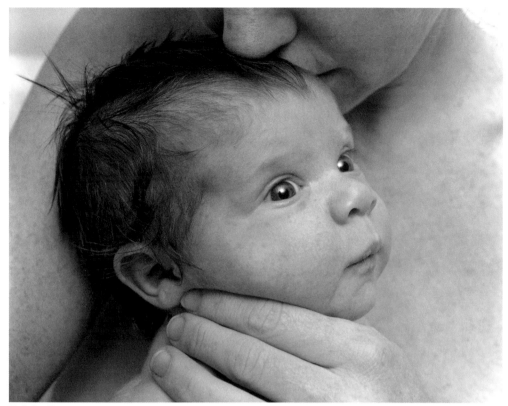

Nicholas Nixon

Nicholas Nixon

Karen Kasmauski

Karen Kasmauski

Alexander Tsiaras

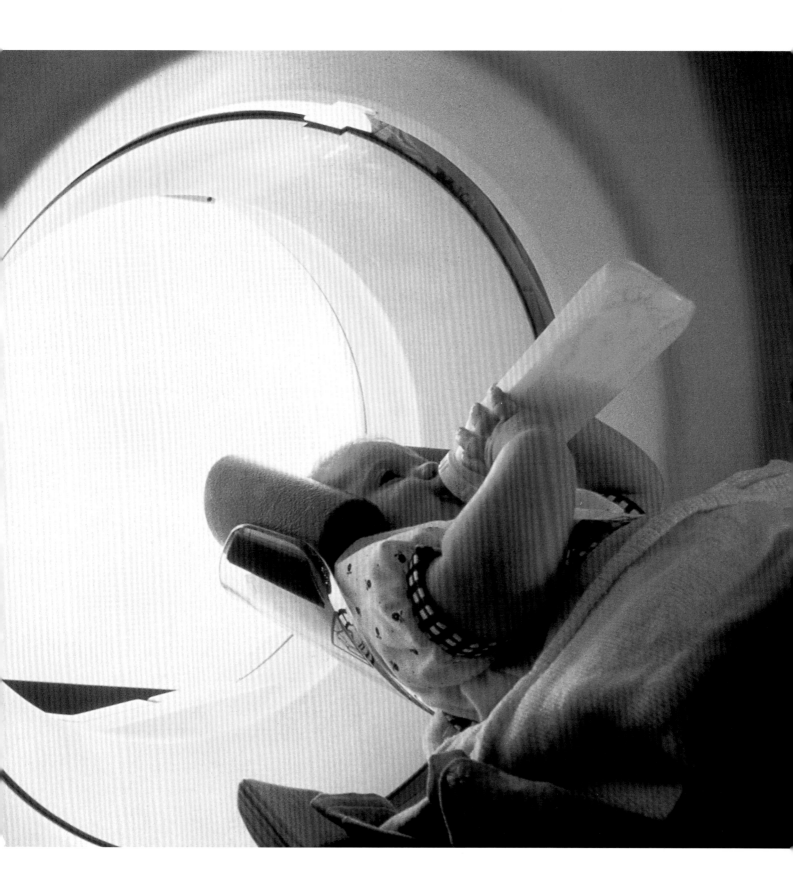

Nicholas DeVore, III

Karl Baden

John Willis

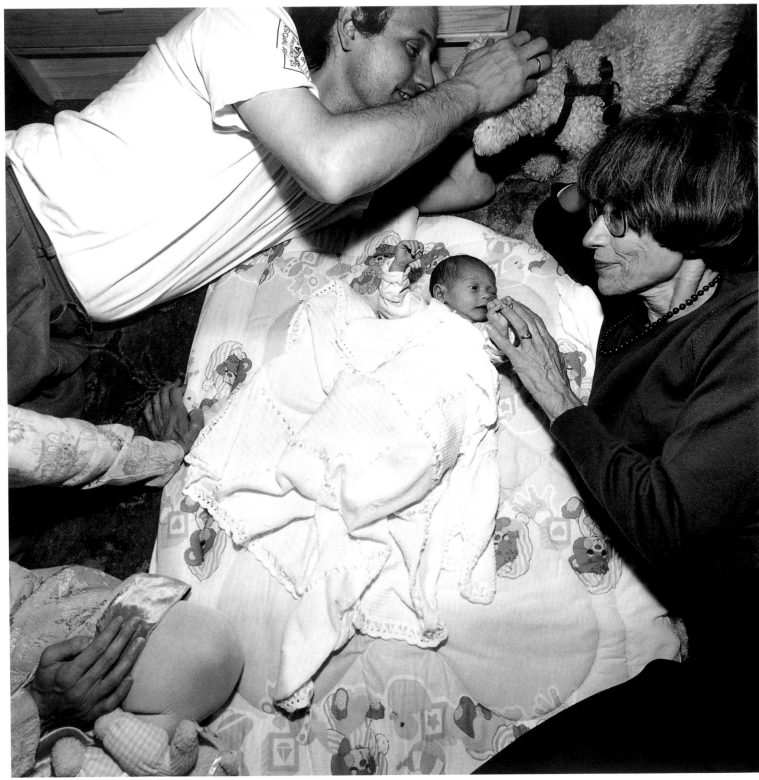

Lee Friedlander

Christine Osinski

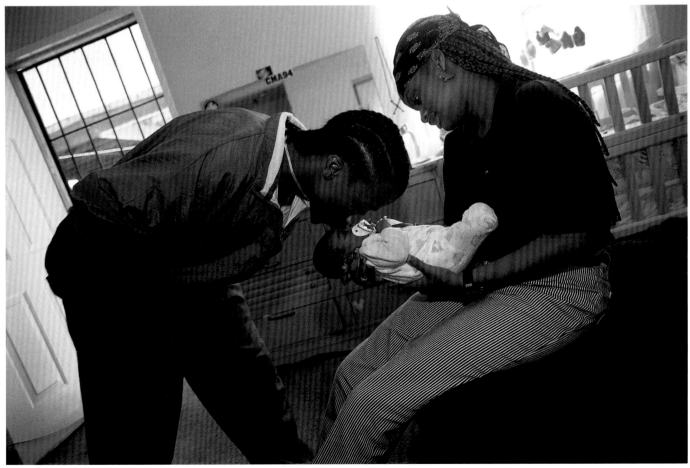

Lauren Greenfield

Tina Barney

Peter Kayafas

Lauren Ronick

Larry Fink

Birney Imes

Susan Meiselas

Geoffrey Biddle

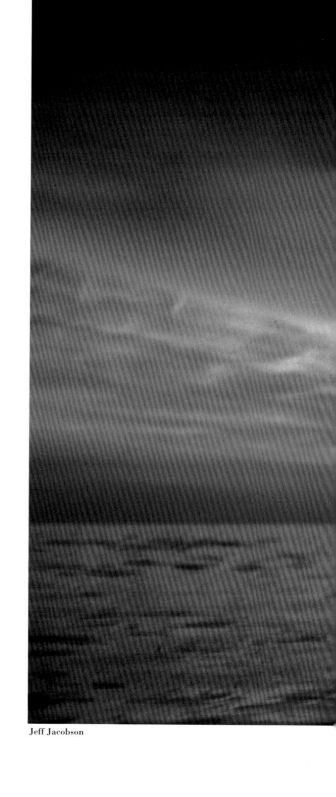
Jeff Jacobson

58

Children are the living messages we send to a time we will not see.

—NEIL POSTMAN

Lee Friedlander

Mitch Epstein

Lauren Ronick

Sage Sohier

Jocelyn Lee

Mary Ellen Mark

Joel Sternfeld

Mitch Epstein

Yunghi Kim

There is always one moment in childhood when the door opens and lets the future in.

—GRAHAM GREENE

Sylvia Plachy

Linda Day Clark

Eugene Richards

Doug DuBois

It is not how much
we do, but how
much love we put in
the doing. It is not
how much we give,
but how much love
we put in the giving.

—MOTHER TERESA

Catherine Opie

Andrea Modica

Cheryl Himmelstein

Melissa Springer

Barbara Norfleet

73

Pamela Duffy

Pamela Duffy

Lauren Ronick

Maude Schuyler Clay

Jennette Williams

following pages: Eugene Richards

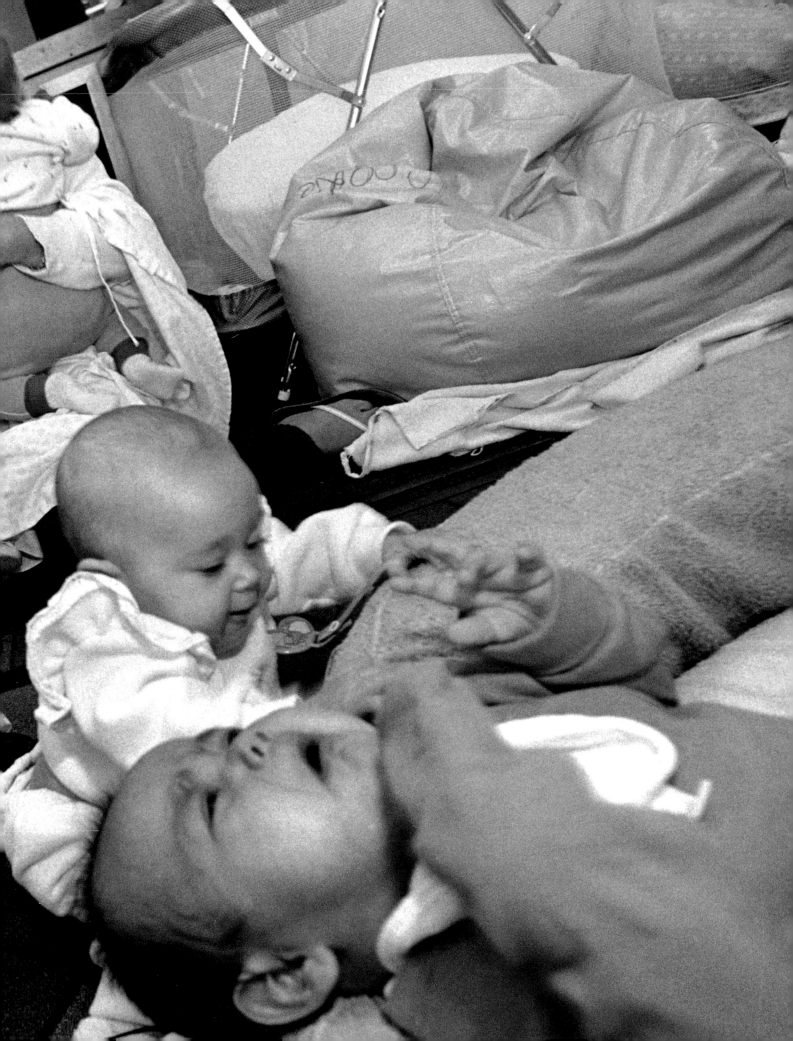

Melissa Ann Pinney

Jennette Williams

Jennette Williams

Larry Fink

Paul D'Amato

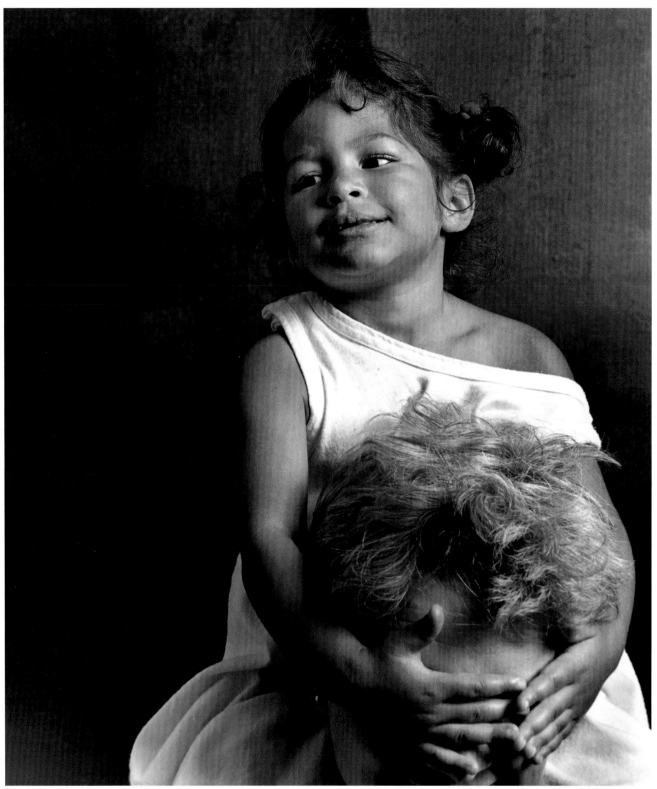

Melissa Springer

The one thing we can never get enough of is love.
And the one thing we never give enough of is love.

—HENRY MILLER

Gerald Cyrus

Paul D'Amato

Jennette Williams

Tyrone Turner

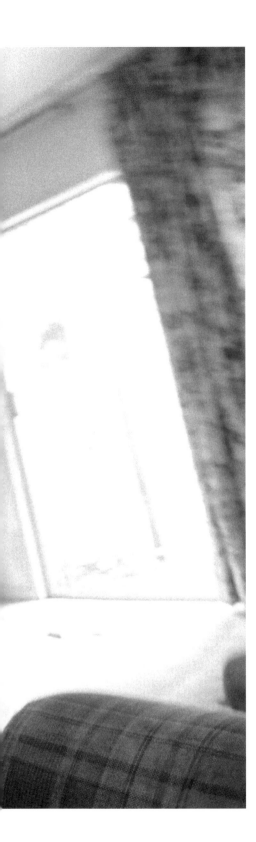

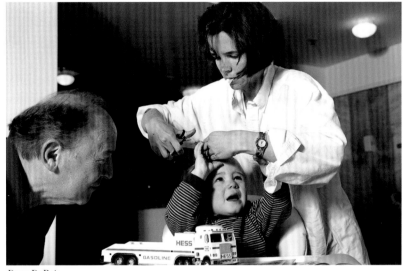

Doug DuBois

Peter Brown

Mary Berridge

Lyle Ashton Harris

Mel Rosenthal

Melissa Ann Pinney

Lee Friedlander

David Hurn

Ken Light

Debbie Fleming Caffery

Jennette Williams

Jennette Williams

Jennette Williams

Jennette Williams

Barbara Norfleet

Jennette Williams

Sylvia Plachy

Lauren Ronick

Gregory Bojorquez

Mitch Epstein

Lauren Greenfield

Joel Sartore

William Albert Allard

Thomas Roma

Mel Rosenthal

Antonio Perez

Lauren Ronick

Here are your waters and your watering place.
Drink and be whole again beyond confusion.

—ROBERT FROST

Birney Imes

Tyrone Turner

David Hurn

Lewis Watts

Tyrone Turner

It is the essential nature of man to play.

— PLATO

Mel Rosenthal

Gerald Cyrus

Joseph Rodriguez

Eli Reed

Sylvia Plachy

Angel Franco

Alice Attie

Lauren Greenfield

Melissa Ann Pinney

Paul D'Amato

Joel Sartore

Arlene Gottfried

Dawoud Bey

Lloyd Ziff

David Graham

Tina Barney

Nicholas Nixon

Sally Mann

Maude Schuyler Clay

My face in thine eye, thine in
    mine appears,
And true plain hearts do in the
    faces rest.

—JOHN DONNE

Nicholas Nixon

Maude Schuyler Clay

Lee Friedlander

David LaChapelle

Lauren Greenfield

Jodi Cobb

Arlene Gottfried

Sage Sohier

Sage Sohier

Sage Sohier

125

Sage Sohier

Sage Sohier

Sage Sohier

Sylvia Plachy

127

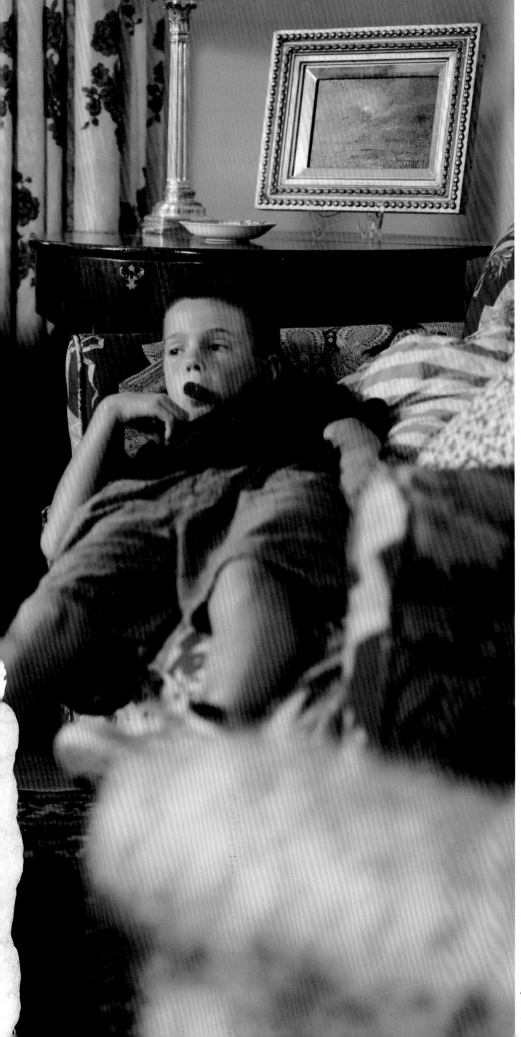

Tina Barney

Melissa Ann Pinney

Gerald Cyrus

Childhood shows the man, as morning shows the day.

—JOHN MILTON

Lauren Greenfield

Eli Reed

Patricia D. Richards

133

Margaret Sartor

Susan Lipper

Joseph Rodriguez

David Alan Harvey

Dana Lixenberg

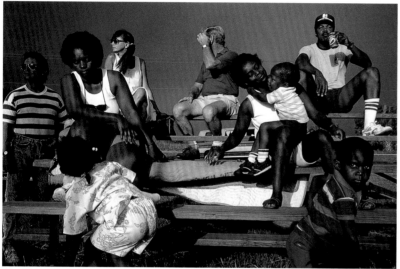

Alex Webb

Gina J. Grillo

Tom Arndt

Justin Kimball

Nan Goldin

Adam Bartos

Alice Attie

Larry Fink

Tina Barney

Wing Young Huie

Jennette Williams

Genaro Molina

The family is the association
established by nature
for the supply
of man's everyday wants.

—ARISTOTLE

Arthur Tress

Marcus Mâm

Larry Fink

Annie Leibovitz

Mitch Epstein

Kenneth Jarecke

Steven Cummings

Larry Sultan

Sage Sohier

Nicholas Nixon

Melissa Ann Pinney

Family faces are magic mirrors. Looking at people who belong to us, we see the past, present and future.

—GAIL LUMET BUCKLEY

Carla Weber

Nicholas Nixon

Nicholas Nixon

Nicholas Nixon

Nicholas Nixon

Peter Goin

Jeff Jacobson

Justin Kimball

162

Justin Kimball

Herbert Randall

Jed Devine

Doug DuBois

Paul D'Amato

Helen Levitt

Alex Webb

Laura Straus

Mary Ellen Mark

Mitch Epstein

Mitch Epstein

Lauren Greenfield

Margaret Morton

Eugene Richards

Larry Sultan

Things which matter most must never be at the mercy of things which matter least.

—JOHANN WOLFGANG VON GOETHE

Eugene Richards

Donna Ferrato

Jane Evelyn Atwood

Donna Ferrato

Alex Webb

Katie Murray

Timothy Fadek

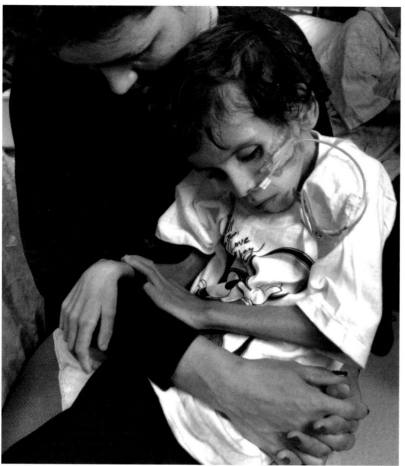
Jack Radcliffe

Make yourself necessary to somebody.

— RALPH WALDO EMERSON

Lori Grinker

Nicholas Nixon

Melissa Ann Pinney

Healthy children will not fear life
if their elders have integrity enough
not to fear death.

—ERIK H. ERIKSON

Sally Mann

Dean Tokuno

188

Dean Tokuno

following pages: Ed Kashi

189

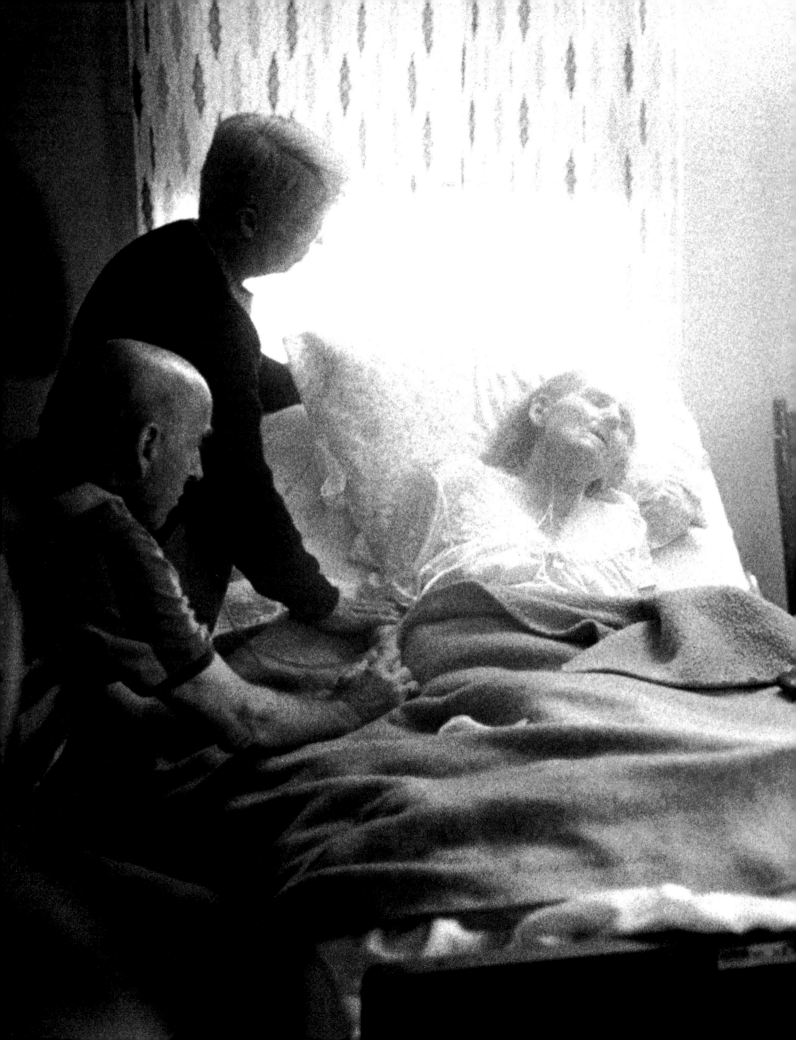

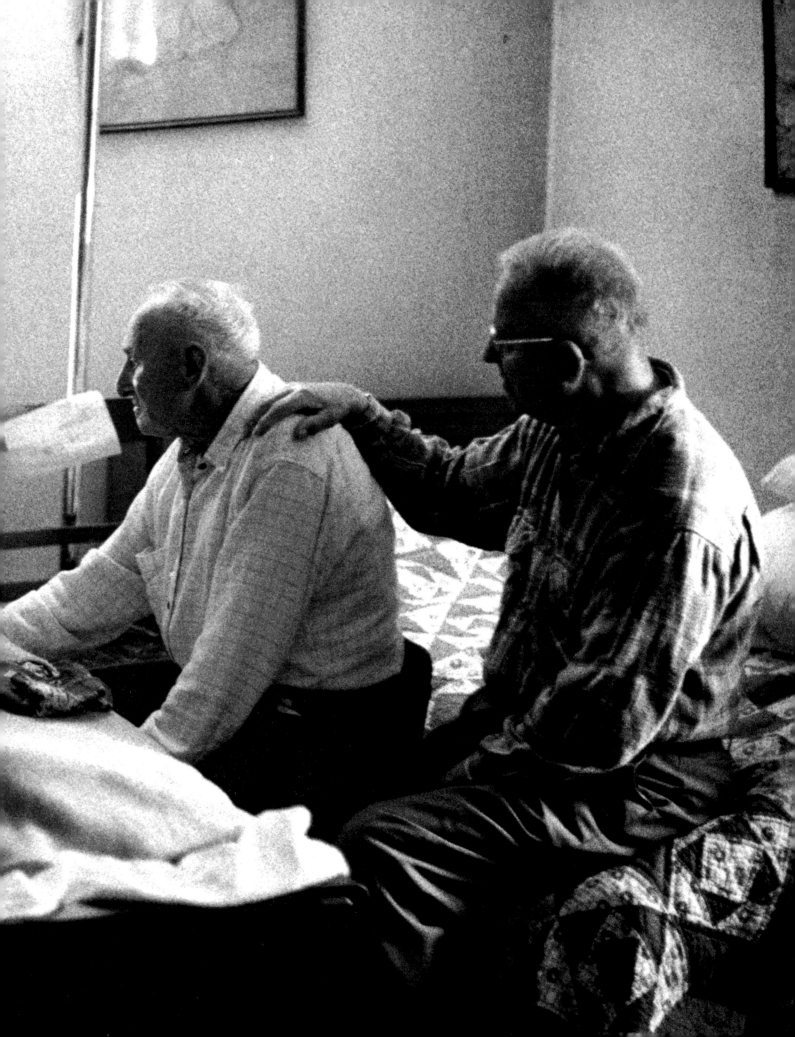

Shelby Lee Adams

Larry Fink

Arlene Gottfried

Larry Fink

David Graham

Elliott Erwitt

Weeping may endure for a night:
but joy cometh in the morning.

—PSALM 30:5

Tom Zimmerman

following pages: Norman Mauskopf

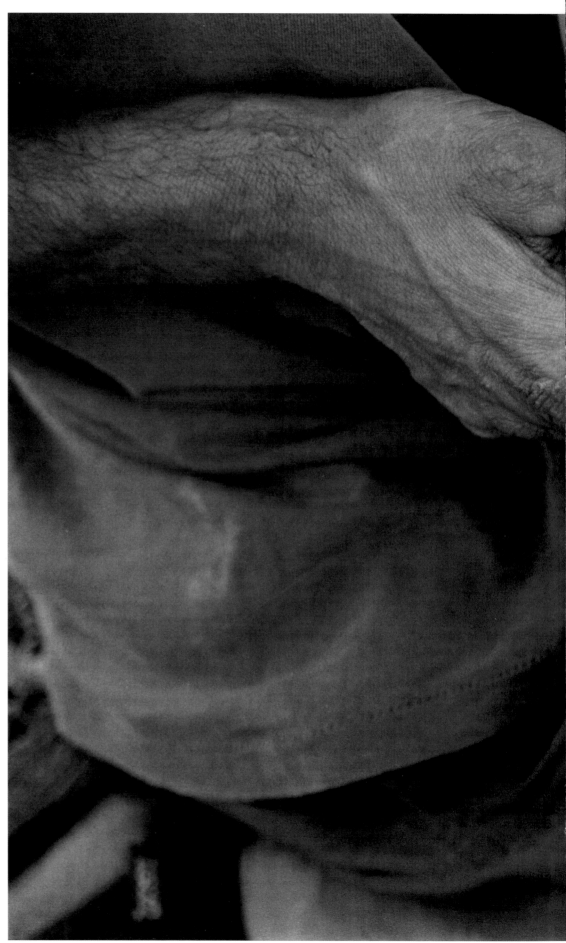

Elliott Erwitt

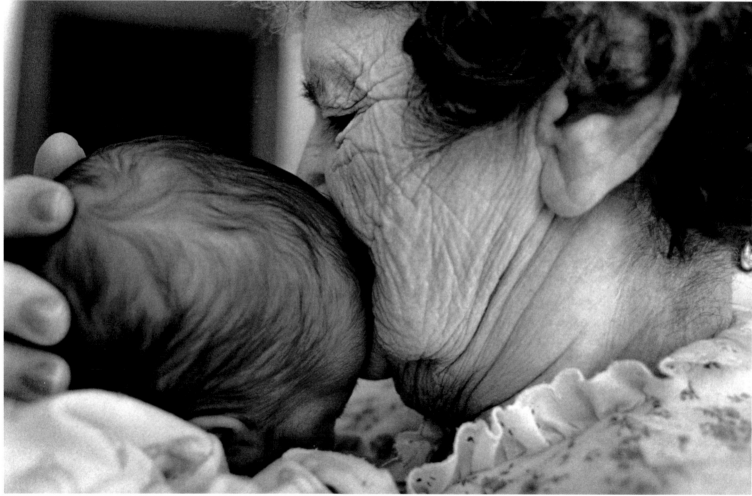

Eugene Richards

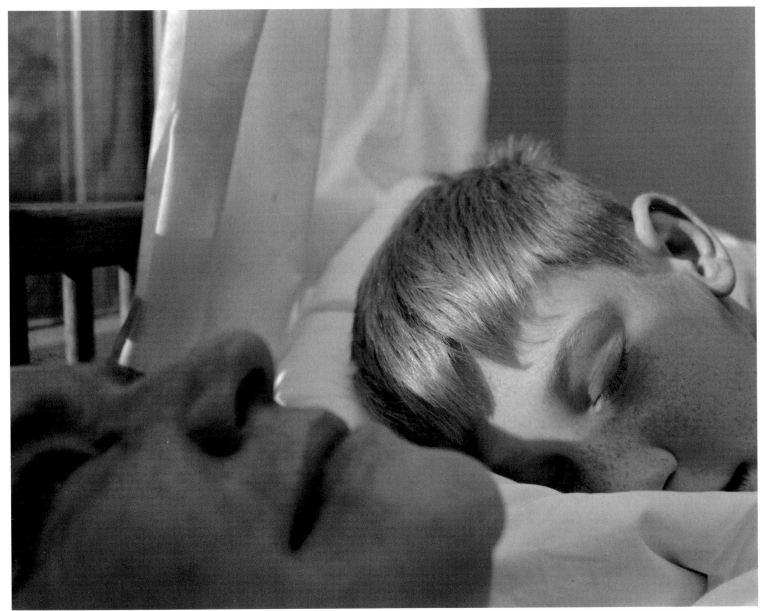

Nicholas Nixon

Sylvia Plachy

Acknowledgments

We wish to express our deep gratitude to the many friends and colleagues who assisted us as we worked to turn our vision for this book into a reality. We thank Jodi Cobb, Chris Johns, Nick Nichols, Bill Allard, and Dave Harvey for the encouragement they gave when this book was just a dream and a concept. Jodi continued to help us enormously every step of the way, and Chris and Nick's advice, guidance, and encouragement throughout the process were invaluable to us. We also want to thank Nancy Rhoda.

It has been a great pleasure to work with Gail Buckland and Katy Homans, whose talents and dedication helped turn this vision into a powerful and emotional book, rich with visual narrative. Gail's and Katy's broad knowledge of the photographic community proved invaluable. Gail is a gifted photographic researcher and editor. Working with photographers from all around the country, she gathered the thousands of wonderful images from which we made our selection. Katy, a brilliant graphic designer, demonstrated an uncanny ability to capture precisely the emotion and mood that we wanted to convey. We consistently relied on her creative eye and sophisticated aesthetic judgment.

Without the wonderful support and cooperation of the photographers represented here, there would be no book. We are indebted to the scores of professionals in the photographic community whose expertise has greatly enhanced the breadth and depth of imagery represented here. In addition to all the photographers, we would like to acknowledge the following individuals for their help in the preparation of the book: Sumaya Agha, June Bateman, Bonni Benrubi, Phil Bloch, Janet Borden, Sabrina Buell, Carolyn Kozo Cole, Phyllis Collazo, Laura Copenhaver, Valdir Cruz, Katherine Culbert-Aguilar, Marisol Diaz, Mitch Epstein,

Wendy Ewald, Lissa Fesus, Peter Gallasi, Wendy Glassmire, Ziggy Golding-Baker, Andy Grundberg, Susan Hertzig, Jenni Holder, Jennifer Hoover, Graham Howe, Barbara Kasten, Deborah Klochko, Kevin Kushel, Katie Lane, Bronwen Latimer, Meredith Lui, Peter MacGill, Ariel Meyerowitz, Laurence Miller, Weston Naef, Robert Pledge, Howard Read, Fred Ritchin, Miriam Romais, Glenna Roth, Melissa Roth, Kathy Ryan, Michael Sand, Gregoire Sauter, Temmie and David Siegal, Michael Shulman, Peter Simmons, Patterson Sims, Robert A. Sobieszek, Jill Sussman, Hank Thomas, David Travis, Ann Wilkes Tucker, Francesca Valerio, Nerissa Vales, Stephen and Mus White, Jennette Williams, Deborah Willis, Jay Wolke, and Amy Woloszyn.

We are grateful to former poet laureate Robert Pinsky for his inspiration as we selected quotations for this book. Our heartfelt thanks to John Sterling and Jennifer Barth at Henry Holt for believing in this book and in our vision of including the widest possible range of work by American photographers. Their many contributions throughout the creative process have been invaluable. We want to acknowledge Andrew Wylie for his assistance in putting this project together. Overflowing gratitude to Audrey Choi for all her advice and, most especially, management of this project. She, along with Dan Taylor and Terry Lumish, made it possible for us to produce this book at the same time we were writing our nonfiction book on family, *Joined at the Heart: The Transformation of the American Family*. We also want to thank Lisa Brown and John Pelosi for their legal expertise and Dwayne Kemp for his support in so many ways. And we always thank our family for their encouragement and support—Karenna and Drew, Kristin, Sarah, and Al.

Shelby Lee Adams, p. 192, *The Home Funeral*, 1990. **William Albert Allard**, pp. 36, 40, 103, courtesy National Geographic Society Image Sales. **Tom Arndt**, pp. 138–9, *Family Watching Rice Street Parade, St. Paul, Minnesota, July 1988.* **Alice Attie**, pp. 4, 110, 141. **Jane Evelyn Atwood**, pp. 178–9, courtesy Contact Press Images. **Karl Baden**, p. 51, *10/22/94 Crown of Toes*, courtesy Robert Mann Gallery. **Anthony Barboza**, p. 37. **Tina Barney**, pp. 54–5, *The Christening*, 1992; p. 115, *Tim, Philip and Phil*, 1993; pp. 128–9, *The Twins*, 1994; pp. 142–3, *The Children's Party*, 1986; all courtesy Janet Borden, Inc. **Adam Bartos**, p. 141, from the "Hither Hills" series, 1991–95. **Mary Berridge**, p. 88, *Lery with Her Children*, from the book *A Positive Life: Portraits of Women Living with HIV* (Running Press, 1997). **Dawoud Bey**, p. 113, *Diamond and Kenneth*, 2001. **Geoffrey Biddle**, p. 58, *Irv and Eve*, 1984. **Gregory Bojorquez**, pp. 25, 100. **Peter Brown**, p. 87, *My Father Being a Dog for Ben, Heath, Massachusetts*, 1982. **Nancy Buirski**, pp. 102–3, from the book *Earth Angels: Migrant Children in America* (Rome Granate Art Books, 1994). **Debbie Fleming Caffery**, p. 35, *Ruth and Dean, Lafayette, Louisiana*, 1995; p. 95, *May Van's Camp, Louisiana*, 1987. **Linda Day Clark**, p. 68, *North Avenue Image No. 30: Babies*, from the "North Avenue, Baltimore" series. **Maude Schuyler Clay**, pp. 75, 117, 120. **Jodi Cobb**, pp. 12–3, 123, courtesy National Geographic Society Image Sales. **Steven Cummings**, p. 150. **Gerald Cyrus**, p. 85, *Mardi Gras Party, New Orleans*, 1993; p. 107, *Boys Playing on Laverne Street, New Orleans*, 1996; p. 131, *Jon and Kamau Dancing, Los Angeles*, 1990. **Paul D'Amato**, p. 40, *Maid of Honor, Chicago*, 1994; p. 83, *Anne and Max, Portland*, 1995; p. 85, *Twister, Chicago*, 1995; p. 111, *Madonna and Esme, Chicago*, 1991; p. 166, *Junior and Janessa, Chicago*, 2000. **Bruce Davidson**, pp. 35, 38–9, courtesy Magnum Photos, Inc. **Jed Devine**, p. 165, *Siobhan, Jessie, Jennifer and Becky Ahlemeyer on Florence Cushman's Wharf/Friendship Long Island, Maine*, courtesy Bonni Benrubi Gallery, NYC. **Nicholas DeVore III**, p. 50, courtesy Allsport/Getty Images. **Doug DuBois**, p. 28, *Donna and Terry, Avella, Pennsylvania*, 1995; pp. 70–1, *Lise and Spencer, New Brunswick, New Jersey*, 1999; p. 87, *My Father, Lise and Spencer, Hoboken, New Jersey*, 2001; p. 166, *My Grandmother and Her Great-Granddaughter, Savannah, Willoughby, Ohio*, 1991. **Pamela Duffy**, both p. 74. **Mitch Epstein**, p. 23, *An-My Lê and John Pilson, New York*, 1998; p. 61, *Susan and Lucia, Goshen*, 2001; p. 66, *Cocoa Beach, Florida*, 1983; pp. 100–1, *Saints Game, Versaille, Louisiana*, 1993; p. 148, *Untitled, New York*, 1997; p. 170, *Untitled, New York*, 1998; p. 171, *Untitled, New York*, 1997; all copyright Black River Productions, Ltd./Mitch Epstein. **Elliot Erwitt**, pp. 195, 198–9, courtesy Magnum Photos, Inc. **Timothy Fadek**, p. 183. **Donna Ferrato**, p. 178, *Boyfriend Arrested for Domestic Assault*, copyright Donna Ferrato/Domestic Abuse Awareness, Inc., from the book *Living with the Enemy* (Aperture, 1991); pp. 180–1, *In the Olive Branch Shelter, a Child Looks for His Mommy.* **Larry Fink**, pp. 57, 82, 142, 147, 192, 193. **Angel Franco**, p. 109, copyright *The New York Times.* **Leonard Freed**, pp. 10–1, courtesy Magnum Photos, Inc. **Lee Friedlander**, pp. 52, 91, 121, all *Untitled*, 1998, courtesy Fraenkel Gallery, San Francisco; p. 60, *Lucia and Susan*, 1998, from the series "Grand Children," courtesy Janet Borden, Inc. **Peter Goin**, pp. 160–1. **Jim Goldberg**, p. 34, *Destiny's Shiny Bracelet*; p. 45, *Echo and Her Mom*, courtesy Pace/MacGill Gallery, New York. **Nan Goldin**, p. 33, *CZ and Max on the Beach, Truro, Massachusetts*, 1975; p. 140, *Picnic on the Esplanade, Boston*, 1972; courtesy Matthew Marks Gallery, New York. **Tipper Gore**, p. 18. **Arlene Gottfried**, pp. 32, 43, 112, 124, 192. **David Graham**, pp. 2–3, 114, 194–5. **Lauren Greenfield**, p. 26, *A High School Sophomore Blows Smoke Into Her Friend's Mouth, Hollywood Boulevard*; p. 53, *Ozzie, 17, and His Girlfriend, Chantel, 17, with Their Newborn, Taylor, in Ozzie's Mother's Home, Where They Live, South Central Los Angeles*; p. 100, *Jenna with Her Doll and Her Father in the Family Room, Encino;* p. 110, *Two Sisters Play with a Friend At the Family Ranch, Malibu*; p. 123, *Jenna, 5, in Her Bedroom with Her Mother, Encino*; p. 132, *Mijanou and Friends from Beverly Hills High School on Senior Beach Day, Will Rogers State Beach*; p. 172, *Candice, 16, and Her Parents in the Living Room of Their New Home, which Candice's Father Designed, Sherman Oaks;* pp. 176–7, *Bryan's Funeral, Rancho Palos Verdes.* **Gina J. Grillo**, p. 138, *Fourth of July, Skokie, Illinois 1997*, from series "Between Cultures: Children of Immigrants in America." **Lori Grinker**, p. 184, courtesy Contact Press Images. **Lyle Ashton Harris**, pp. 88–9, *Mary Ann Moore and Children*, 1994. **David Alan Harvey**, p. 136, courtesy Magnum Photos, Inc. **Cheryl Himmelstein**, p. 73. **Wing Young Huie**, p. 144, *Hmong Women at the Table, Frogtown, St. Paul, Minnesota.* **David Hurn**, pp. 46, 92–3, 106, courtesy Magnum Photos, Inc. **Birney Imes**, p. 22, *Girl on Catfish Alley*; p. 58, *Isola, Mississippi*; p. 105, *Oaklimb Baptism*; courtesy Bonni Benrubi Gallery, NYC. **Jeff Jacobson**, pp. 58–9, 161. **Kenneth Jarecke**, pp. 26–7, 148–9, courtesy Contact Press Images. **Ed Kashi**, pp. 190–1. **Karen Kasmauski**, p. 48, both from the Human Genome project, courtesy Matrix International, Inc. **Peter Kayafas**, p. 56, *Greek Orthodox Baptism, Washington, D.C., 1992.* **Edward Keating**, p. 40, copyright *The New York Times.* **Ruth Kendrick**, p. 25, *Richie and Brian, Spring 1993, New York City.* **Yunghi Kim**, p. 66, courtesy Contact Press Images. **Justin Kimball**, p. 29, *Cape Cod, Massachusetts*, 1997; p. 140, *Greenfield, Massachusetts*, 1997; p. 162, *Point Judith, Rhode Island*, 1997; p. 163, *Tremont, Indiana*, 1997. **David LaChapelle**, p. 122, *Miss Coney Island Beauty Pageant*, courtesy Staley+Wise Gallery, New York. **Jocelyn Lee**, p. 64, *Leander, Texas*, 1992. **Laura Letinsky**, p. 36, *Untitled (Laura and Eric)*, 1993, from the "Venus Inferred" series, courtesy Edwynn Houk Gallery, New York. **Helen Levitt**, p. 166, courtesy Laurence Miller Gallery, New York. **Annie Leibovitz**, p. 148, courtesy Contact Press Images. **Ken Light**, p. 94. **Susan Lipper**, p. 135, from the "Grapevine" series. **Dana Lixenberg**, p. 137, from the story "That Other Island," a visual portrait of Staten Island, courtesy Z Photographic. **Marcus Mâm**, pp. 146–7, *Three People Eating Ribs*, courtesy Leyla Basakinci Inc. **Sally Mann**, p. 42, *Untitled*, 1984; p. 116, *Larry Shaving*, 1991; pp. 186–7, *He is Very Sick*, 1986; all courtesy Edwynn Houk Gallery, New York. **Constantine Manos**, pp. 30–1, courtesy Magnum Photos, Inc. **Malerie Marder**, pp. 24–5, courtesy Artemis Greenberg Van Doren Fine Art. **Mary Ellen Mark**, p. 7, *Brooklyn, New York*, 2001; p. 65, *Jennifer Holding Baby Tiffany*; p. 169, *Homeless Family in Car.* **Norman Mauskopf**, pp. 196–7, courtesy Matrix International, Inc. **Susan Meiselas**, pp. 29, 58, courtesy Magnum Photos, Inc. **Duane Michals**, p. 9, *The Seven Stages of Man*, courtesy Pace/MacGill Gallery, New York. **Andrea Modica**, p. 72, courtesy Marilyn Cadenbach Associates. **Genaro Molina**, p. 145, copyright *Los Angeles Times.* **Abelardo Morell**, pp. 16–7, *Laura and Brady in the Shadow of Our House*, 1994, courtesy Bonni Benrubi Gallery, NYC. **Margaret Morton**, pp. 172–3, Ombra Luce LLC © 1993. **Katie Murray**, p. 182, *Family Watching TV September 11.* **James Newberry**, p. 6, *Palestinian-American Family at Home*, 1988. **Nicholas Nixon**, p. 47 (top), *Clementine, Cambridge*, 1985; p. 47 (bottom), *Bebe and Clementine, Cambridge*, 1985; p. 116, *Yazoo City, Mississippi*, 1979; pp. 118–9, *Bebe and Clementine, Lexington*, 1995; p. 154, *Emma Street, Lakeland, Florida*, 1982; p. 158 (top), *The Brown Sisters*, 1983; p. 158 (bottom), *The Brown Sisters*, 1990; p. 159 (top), *The Brown Sisters*, 1998; p. 159 (bottom), *The Brown Sisters*, 1999; p. 185, *Tom Moran and His Mother, Catherine Moran, August 1987*; p. 201; *Bebe and Sam, Cambridge*, 1995. **Barbara P. Norfleet**, pp. 73, *Grandchildren*; 98, *Grandchildren.* **Catherine Opie**, p. 28, *Tammy Rae and Kaia, Durham, North Carolina*, 1998; p. 72, *Joanne, Betsy and Olivia, Bayside, New York*, 1998; both from the "Domestic" series, courtesy Gorney Bravin + Lee, New York and Regen Projects, Los Angeles. **Christine Osinski**, p. 53. **Antonio Perez**, p. 104. **Melissa Ann Pinney**, p. 80, *Disney World*, 1998; p. 90, *Kiara and Emma, Evanston, Illinois*, 2001; p. 111, *Sisters, Illinois State Fair*, 1999; pp. 130–1, *Bat Mitzvah Dance, Knickerbocker Hotel, Chicago*, 1991; p. 155, *Ice Cream Social, Evanston, Illinois*, 2001, p. 186, *Barbara and Vivian.* **Sylvia Plachy**, pp. 67, 98–9, 109, photographed for the *New Yorker*; pp. 127, 203. **Jack Radcliffe**, p. 184. **Herbert Randall**, pp. 164–5. **Eli Reed**, pp. 26, 108–9, 132, courtesy Magnum Photos, Inc. **Eugene Richards**, pp. 42, 69, 78–9, 178, 200, courtesy Magnum Photos, Inc. **Patricia D. Richards**, p. 133, *Making Up.* **Joseph Rodriguez**, pp. 106–7, *Girl with Hoola Hoop*; p. 135, *Chivo Teaches His Daughter.* **Milton Rogovin**, p. 14, *Triptych 1973, 1985, 1992*; p. 152, *Triptych 1974, 1986, 1992.* **Thomas Roma**, p. 104, from the book *Come Sunday* (The Museum of Modern Art/Harry N. Abrams, 1994). **Lauren Ronick**, pp. 56, 62, 74, 99, 104. **Mel Rosenthal**, p. 88, *Mother and Daughter Near State Street, Syracuse*, 1992; p. 104, *Arab-American Fathers and Sons, Bay Ridge, Brooklyn*, 2000; p. 107, *Palestinian-American Rollerblading on 4th Avenue, Bay Ridge, Brooklyn*, 1999. **Margaret Sartor**, p. 134, *Cowboys and Indians, Durham, North Carolina*, 1994. **Joel Sartore**, pp. 102, 112, courtesy Joel Sartore/www.joelsartore.com. **Sage Sohier**, pp. 63, 124, 125, 126, 127, 152–3. **Melissa Springer**, pp. 73, 84. **Joel Sternfeld**, p. 30, *High School Prom at the Hilton, San Antonio, Texas, April 1999*; p. 65, *A Man with a Training Baby, Beckley, West Virginia, May 1999*, courtesy Pace/MacGill Gallery, New York. **Laura Straus**, p. 41, *African American Wedding*, photograph provided courtesy of New Line Television, Inc.™ and © 2002. All rights reserved; p. 168, *Parents and Three Daughters.* **Larry Sultan**, pp. 150–1, 174–5, courtesy Z Photographic. **Hank Thomas** and **Bayeté Ross-Smith**, p. 14–5. **Dean Tokuno**, pp. 188, 189. **Arthur Tress**, p. 145, courtesy Magnum Photos, Inc. **Alexander Tsiaras**, pp. 48–9, courtesy Science Source/Photo Researchers. **Toba Pato Tucker**, p. 8, *Rose Naranjo and Family, Santa Clara Pueblo, New Mexico.* **Tyrone Turner**, pp. 86–7, 106, 106–7, courtesy Black Star. **Lewis Watts**, pp. 106–7, *Martin Luther King Way, West Oakland*, 1993. **Alex Webb**, pp. 138, 166–7, 182, courtesy Magnum Photos, Inc. **Carla Weber**, pp. 156–7. **Jennette Williams**, pp. 76–7, *Central Park West Annunciation (Vernour, Emmet, and Peatree), New York City*, 1993; pp. 80–1, *Rabbit Ears*, 1993; p. 81, *After the Waterpark with Cami, Riverhead, New York*, 1994; p. 85, *First Birthday*, 1990; p. 96 (top), *Emmet on the Telephone, New York City*, 1992; p. 96 (bottom), *First Swim Lesson*, 1993; p. 97 (top), *Abby in the Kitchen*, 1994; p. 97 (bottom), *Emmet and Teddy with Water Guns*, 1994; pp. 98–9, *Passover*, 1999; p. 144, *Thanksgiving, Glen Head, New York*, 1990. **John Willis**, p. 51. **Laura Wilson**, p. 5, *The Waldner Family* from the book *Hutterites of Montana* (Yale University Press, 2001). **Lloyd Ziff**, p. 114, *Father and Son*, 1979. **Tom Zimmerman**, p. 195, *While the Band Played "Jambalaya," Creole Celebration, Verbum Dei High School, Los Angeles*, 1990.

About the Authors

Al Gore, forty-fifth Vice President of the United States, was a journalist in Tennessee and in the U.S. Army, including service in Vietnam. In 1976, he won a seat in the U.S. House of Representatives; he was elected to the U.S. Senate in 1984. During his many years of public service, he has made the American family a priority by working for new solutions that address needs of families and communities. Al Gore is the author of the *New York Times* bestseller *Earth in the Balance*. He is now a professor at both Fisk University and Middle Tennessee State University, where he teaches "Family-Centered Community Building," a course he also teaches part-time at UCLA. Together with his wife, Tipper, he created their annual two-day policy forum called "Family Re-Union," now in its eleventh year. They have four children and two grand-children, and they live in Nashville, Tennessee.

Al Gore was born on March 31, 1948, and raised in both Carthage, Tennessee, and Washington, D.C. He received a degree in government with honors from Harvard University in 1969, and attended Vanderbilt University's Divinity School and Law School.

Tipper Gore is known worldwide as an advocate for families, women, and children, and is actively involved in issues related to mental health, education, and the homeless. From 1993 to 2001, she served as Advisor to the President on Mental Health Policy and chaired the first White House Conference on Mental Health. In 2000, she formed the National Mental Health Awareness Campaign and currently serves as its Honorary Chair. Formerly a photojournalist for *The Tennessean*, in 1988 she launched a major photographic exhibit, *Homeless in America*, to put a human face on the national statistics of homelessness. Ten years later, she both chaired and contributed her own work for a traveling photographic exhibit and book, *The Way Home*. She also initiated a national public awareness campaign, spearheaded by the National Alliance to End Homelessness. She is the author of two books: *Raising PG Kids in an X-Rated Society* and *Picture This*, a collection of her photographs.

Born Mary Elizabeth Aitcheson on August 19, 1948, Tipper Gore grew up in Arlington, Virginia. She received a bachelor of arts degree in psychology from Boston University in 1970 and a master's degree in psychology from the George Peabody College of Vanderbilt University in 1975.

About the Collaborators

Gail Buckland is the author of nine photographic books including *The Magic Image* with Cecil Beaton; *Fox Talbot and the Invention of Photography*; and, most recently, *Shots in the Dark: True Crime Pictures*. She collaborated with Harold Evans on *The American Century*, published in 1998. She is an associate professor of the history of photography at the Cooper Union, New York City. A graduate of the University of Rochester, she is the mother of Alaina and Kevin.

Katy Homans is a graphic designer who has specialized in art and photography books for the past thirty years. She has designed books for many of the photographers in *The Spirit of Family*, including Tina Barney, Elliott Erwitt, Lee Friedlander, Nicholas Nixon, Barbara Norfleet, Eli Reed, Milton Rogovin, Larry Sultan, and Jennette Williams. Her work is included in the collection of the Museum of Modern Art. A graduate of Harvard and Yale, she is the mother of Mardet and Lally.

Henry Holt and Company, LLC
Publishers since 1866
115 West 18th Street
New York, New York 10011

Grateful acknowledgment for permission to reprint previously published material
is made to the following:
Line from "For a Child Expected" copyright © 1994 by Anne Ridler, from
Collected Poems, reprinted by permission of Carcanet Press, Ltd.
Line from "Wreath for a Bridal" from *The Collected Poems of Sylvia Plath*, edited by
Ted Hughes. Copyright © 1960, 1965, 1971, 1981 by the Estate of Sylvia Plath.
Editorial material copyright © 1981 by Ted Hughes. Reprinted by permission of
HarperCollins Publishers Inc.
First stanza of "There is a sacred, secret line in loving" by Anna Akhmatova,
translated from the Russian by Jane Kenyon, copyright 1999 by the Estate of
Jane Kenyon. Reprinted from *A Hundred White Daffodils* with the permission of
Graywolf Press, Saint Paul, Minnesota.
Excerpt from "Directive" by Robert Frost from *The Poetry of Robert Frost*, edited
by Edward Connery Lathem. Copyright 1947, © 1969 by Henry Holt and Co.,
© 1975 by Lesley Frost Ballantine. Reprinted by arrangement with Henry Holt
and Company, LLC.

Library of Congress Cataloging-in-Publication data is available.
ISBN: 0-8050-6894-5

First Edition 2002

Designed by Katy Homans

Printed in Singapore
10 9 8 7 6 5 4 3 2 1